Twelfth Night

A Shakespeare Story

RETOLD BY ANDREW MATTHEWS
ILLUSTRATED BY TONY ROSS

ORCHARD

To Sue, with love
A.M.

For Toby K.
T.R.

ORCHARD BOOKS
338 Euston Road, London NW1 3BH
Orchard Books Australia
Hachette Children's Books
Level 17/207 Kent St, Sydney, NSW 2000
This text was first published in Great Britain in the form of a gift collection
called The Orchard Book of Shakespeare Stories, illustrated by
Angela Barrett in 2001.
This edition first published in hardback in Great Britain in 2002
First paperback publication in 2003
This slipcase edition published in 2013
Not for individual resale
Text © Andrew Matthews 2001
Illustrations © Tony Ross 2002
ISBN 978 1 40780 984 7
The rights of Andrew Matthews to be identified as the author and Tony Ross as
the illustrator of this work have been asserted by them in accordance with the
Copyright, Designs and Patents Act, 1988
A CIP catalogue record for this book is available from the British Library
Printed in China

Orchard Books is a division of Hachette Childrens Books,
an Hachette UK company.
www.hachette.co.uk

Contents

Cast List

Sebastian and Viola

Twin brother and sister

Olivia

A rich Countess

Orsino

Duke of Illyria

Malvolio
Steward to Olivia

Sir Toby Belch
Uncle to Olivia

Sir Andrew Aguecheek
Friend to Sir Toby

A Sailor

The Scene
Coastal Illyria, fifteenth century.

If music be the food of love, play on,
Give me excess of it,

Orsino; I.i.

Twelfth Night

Sebastian and his twin sister Viola were as alike as two raindrops. They had the same light brown hair, bright blue eyes and winning smiles. Sometimes, when they were children, Viola used to borrow Sebastian's clothes and pretend to be him – which confused everybody.

The twins grew up together, were taught together, and they almost died together. That was on the day the ship in which they were travelling foundered on a treacherous

reef and sank. Viola saved herself by clinging to Sebastian's clothes-trunk, and was washed up on the coast of Illyria.

As she was a practical, quick-thinking person, Viola decided she would be safer if she disguised herself as a young man, so she tied up her hair, dressed in clothes that she took from her brother's trunk and called herself Cesario. She prayed that Sebastian had survived the shipwreck and for three days she sought news of him, but then her money ran out, so, still disguised as Cesario, she found a job as a page to Duke Orsino, ruler of Illyria.

Orsino was delighted with his new page, and before long, Viola had won his confidence, and he had won her heart. The Duke was tall, dark, handsome, rich, and popular with his people – and yet he was not content. He moped about his palace during the day, and in the evening listened to troubadours singing sad songs. He never laughed, and hardly ever smiled.

Like many young
women before her,
Viola found herself
falling in love with
Orsino and it was
painful to keep her
feelings a secret. The
pain became even worse

when, one day when they were alone
together, she summoned
up the courage to
ask why he was
so unhappy.
"Because
I am suffering
from the worst
sickness in the
world – love!"
Orsino replied.

"I'm so in love with Countess Olivia that I don't know what to do, Cesario! I've asked her to marry me a dozen times, but she keeps refusing."

"She must be mad!" said Viola. "If you asked me to – I mean, if I were a woman, I would marry you at once, my lord!"

Orsino sighed, then suddenly he had an idea that seemed so brilliant, that for a moment he looked almost happy. "You know, Cesario, I think you could gain Olivia's trust as quickly as you have gained mine," he said thoughtfully. "Go and see her today. Tell her that if she won't marry me, I'll waste away and die!"

"Me, my lord?" gulped Viola.

Orsino placed his hand on Viola's shoulder. "You're my last hope!"

'So I must try and persuade Countess Olivia to marry the man I love!' Viola thought ruefully. 'Why does life have to be so complicated?'

Though she did not realise it at that moment, Viola's life was about to become more complicated than she could possibly imagine.

Countess Olivia's
parents had died
when she was
still young and
her uncle, Sir
Toby Belch, had
come to live with her.
Sir Toby was short and
plump, with white whiskers and twinkling
blue eyes, and his love of wine and good

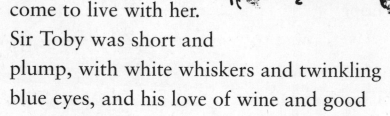

food had turned his nose
bright red. His
closest friend
was Sir Andrew
Aguecheek, a
man with a
face as long
and wrinkled as
a bloodhound's.

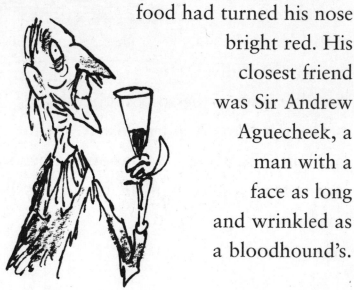

Since Sir Andrew was a bachelor, Sir Toby had decided that he would make the perfect husband for his niece, Olivia. However, Olivia's steward, Malvolio, protected her from all unwanted suitors, including Sir Andrew!

On the day that Orsino sent Viola to plead with Olivia, Sir Toby and Sir Andrew were plotting together in the library of Olivia's house.

"If I could only be alone with her for five minutes!" Sir Andrew grumbled. "But Malvolio will not let me see her. He won't even give her my letters."

"My niece has given him far too much control of her affairs, and it's gone to his head," grumbled Sir Tony. "Why, the other evening, the scoundrel actually had the impudence to tell me that I drink too much!"

"The villain!" said Sir Andrew.

"But I intend to teach him a lesson," Sir Toby said, with a mischievous grin. "Mark my words, old friend, before the day is over, Malvolio will be out of your way."

While her uncle schemed in the library,
Olivia was strolling in the garden with
Malvolio at her side. With his skinny
body and black clothes, Malvolio
resembled a bony shadow. "A young man
called Cesario wishes to see you, my
lady," he was saying to her. "He brings a
message from the Duke Orsino."

"Tell him to go away!" said Olivia, and her green eyes flashed as she tossed her dark-red hair in irritation.

"I have, my lady," said Malvolio. "But he says he will stand at the gate all afternoon if he has to." Malvolio sniffed haughtily. "He is a most insolent young fellow!"

"Oh, let me see him, then!" Olivia said wearily. "Perhaps, when he hears my reply, Orsino will finally abandon all hope of marrying me!"

When Viola entered the garden, Olivia pretended to be interested in the blossoms on a rose bush, and gave Orsino's new messenger no more than a glance.

"Sweet lady," said Viola. "Now I see how beautiful you are, I understand why my master is so in love with you!" Olivia, who hated flattery of any kind, snorted scornfully. "Beautiful?" she said. "I have two eyes, a nose and a mouth like everybody else, if that's what you mean!"

"Ah, so you are proud as well as lovely!" said Viola. "It is a pity that the Duke loves a lady with such a hard heart."

"Orsino doesn't really love me!" Olivia declared. "He's just in love with the idea of being in love. Go and tell him I cannot make myself love him just because he wants me to!" She looked up from the roses, and as she did so, she saw quite the most beautiful young man she had ever met.

Her head swam giddily and her heart began to pound. "Tell Orsino that I will never marry him," she said breathlessly.

"And then...
come back
to see me at
once, Cesario."
"Why?"
frowned Viola.
"Er...to tell me
how he responds
to my answer!"
Olivia said with a blush.

Viola bowed and turned to go, leaving
Olivia alone with a whirlwind of thoughts
and feelings she had never experienced
before. One moment, Olivia wanted to
laugh out loud, and the next, she wanted
to burst into tears. She was so confused,
that she did not notice Malvolio
approaching. He seemed to drop out of
the sky and land in front of her.

"I hope that young man did not offend you, my lady?" Malvolio said.

"Offend me?" said Olivia. "Why, no. I mean – yes, yes he did!" On impulse, she pulled a ring from one of her fingers. "He brought me this gift from the Duke. Return the ring to Cesario and tell him I don't want it!"

"Of course, my lady," Malvolio said smoothly. "Where is the fellow?"

"Gone," said Olivia. "If you run, you'll soon catch up with him."

"What, run – I?" gasped Malvolio; then he bowed politely as he saw the angry green fire in Olivia's eyes. "I'll go at once!" he said.

Viola walked slowly. Her heart was heavy for Orsino, and herself, and when a voice from behind called out, "Cesario?" for a moment she forgot that it was the name she had given herself, and did not remember until the voice called out again. "Cesario! Ho, there!"

Viola turned and saw Malvolio running towards her, his elbows sticking out and his knobbly knees pumping up and down. This was surprise enough, but Viola was completely astonished when Malvolio offered her a ring. "You brought my lady this!" he panted. "Now she wants you to take it back."

"I didn't give her a ring!" said Viola.

Malvolio peevishly stamped his foot and threw the ring to the ground. "Let it lie there, then!" he snapped. "I have better things to do than argue with the likes of you!" He turned on his heel and marched angrily away.

Viola stooped and picking up the ring, saw on it a design of two hands holding a heart. 'But this is a love token!' she thought. 'Young women don't send love tokens to other young women!' The truth fell on her like an avalanche. "Oh, no!" she cried. "Olivia thinks I'm a man – and she's fallen in love with me!"

Orsino was alone when Viola found him. He was singing a song about doomed lovers and how, no matter how brightly the sun shone, somewhere the rain was sure to be pouring down like tears. Viola waited until the song was over, then told Orsino what Olivia had said.

Orsino closed his eyes. "Ah!" he groaned tragically. "If you knew what agony love can be, Cesario!"

"Oh, I do, my lord!" Viola said.

Orsino unpinned a brooch from his doublet and handed it to Viola. "Then go to Olivia again," he said. "Give her this brooch and tell her that even though she will not be my wife, my love will last as long as the diamonds that are set into it!"

* * *

Meanwhile Malvolio had returned to the garden. Olivia was not there, but as he hurried towards the house to find her, he found a letter lying on the path and picked it up.

"Why, this is my lady's handwriting!"
Malvolio murmured. "Since I am her
steward, and her business is my business,
it is my duty to read it!" He was so
interested in the letter that he failed to
see Sir Toby and Sir Andrew, hidden in a
bank of laurel bushes nearby.

"*To M, my dearest love,*" Malvolio read aloud. "*Though you are my servant, you are master of my heart. Be bold, and my hand is yours! If you love me, wear yellow tights, cross-gartered, as a secret sign.*" Malvolio clutched the letter to his bosom. "Olivia loves me!" he burbled. "I must change into yellow tights at once!"

As soon as Malvolio was out of sight, the laurel bushes began to shake with laughter. "I knew it would work!" Sir Toby told Sir Andrew. "I can imitate my niece's handwriting well enough to deceive anybody! Now all we have to do is..."

"Hush!" said Sir Andrew. "Someone is coming!"

Olivia and Viola were deep in conversation. They stopped in front of a bank of laurel bushes, and Viola said, "Then you have no new answer for the Duke?"

"No!" said Olivia, clutching Viola's hand. "But there are answers I would give to you, Cesario, if you would only ask me the questions!"

Viola gently took her hand away. "My lady, I am not all that I seem to be," she said tactfully.

"But I love you!" exclaimed Olivia. "I loved you from the first moment I set eyes on you."

"You might as well love a dream," Viola said. "You must forget me, my lady!" and she slipped away, leaving Olivia in tears.

In the bushes, Sir Andrew quivered with rage. "That chit of a youth has stolen Olivia's love!" he hissed.

"After him!" urged Sir Toby. "Challenge him to a duel! That should see him off!"

"A duel?" said Sir Andrew, alarmed.

"He won't dare to fight you!" said Sir Toby. "That Cesario is nothing but a puny milksop – he'll turn tail and run the moment you draw your sword!"

✳ ✳ ✳

While Sir Andrew went to waylay Viola at
the garden gate, Olivia stumbled towards
the house, her eyes filled with tears. "Oh,
Cesario!" she whispered. "I must see you
again, if only for a second!"

Then she saw Malvolio walking towards her. He was wearing yellow tights as bright as canaries, and his face was stretched into a ghastly smile. "Well met, my angel!" he simpered.

"Malvolio?" said Olivia. "Are you feeling quite well?"

"Never better, my sweetness!" Malvolio purred, stretching out his leg. "Have you noticed my yellow tights and cross-garters?"

"I could hardly miss them!" Olivia replied. "I think the heat has made you feverish. Wouldn't you like to lie down?"

"Yes, with you by my side!" said
Malvolio.

"Help!" cried Olivia. "Servants, take
Malvolio away! He has lost his wits!"

* * *

Meanwhile, Viola, relieved to be going back to her master, the Duke, suddenly found herself face to face with a furious Sir Andrew Aguecheek.

"Draw your sword, vile scoundrel!" snarled Sir Andrew.

"My sword?" Viola quailed. "But why?"

"So I can fight you!" Sir Andrew said. "Or are you a coward as well as a villain?"

Reluctantly, Viola reached for her sword with a trembling hand, and at that same moment, most fortunately a loud voice shouted, "Stop!"

A hefty sailor appeared through the gateway.

"If you harm one hair of this young man's head," he warned Sir Andrew, "I'll carve you up like a joint of beef!"

"Oh!" said Sir Andrew, pale with fear. "Oh, well in that case, I think I'd better..." and he ran away at an impressive speed.

Viola felt weak with relief. "How can I ever thank you, kind stranger?" she said to the sailor.

"Stranger?" scowled the sailor. "That's a fine thing to call the man who saved you from drowning and helped you to try and find your lost sister! I've been waiting for you at the inn down the road for the last two days, Sebastian!"

"*Sebastian?*" gasped Viola. "Then my brother is alive and well!"

✳ ✳ ✳

Sebastian was alive and well, but totally
bewildered. On his way to meet the sailor
who had saved him, he happened to pass
a fine house out of which rushed
a beautiful red-haired
young woman. "I
knew you would
come back, Cesario!"
she said, flinging
her arms around
him. "We cannot
live without
each other!"

"But, my lady,"
Sebastian said.

"Call me Olivia,
my dearest!"
said Olivia.

Sebastian looked into Olivia's eyes. He was about to tell her that she had made a terrible mistake, and that his name was not Cesario, but

then his heart began to beat faster as love

worked its magic on him. "This must be a dream!" he said softly. "But please, don't wake me up yet!" And he hugged Olivia tightly.

The two of them were still embracing when Viola and the sailor discovered them. Sebastian recognised his sister and ran to her with a joyous shout. He lifted Viola high into the air, while Olivia and the sailor looked on open-mouthed.

"Are there two of him?" whispered
Olivia. "I don't understand."

"It seems so," said the sailor, scratching
his head. "If you ask me, my lady,
someone has a lot of explaining to do!"

* * *

Duke Orsino waited two anxious hours
for Cesario to return, and at last he lost
his patience. He called for his fastest
horse, and galloped to Olivia's house.

In the hall, he was met with the strangest
sight – Cesario and Olivia, arm in arm,
and behind them, a smiling priest holding
a bible.

"Cesario!" Orsino thundered. "Release
that lady!"

"This is not Cesario, my lord," Olivia beamed. "This is Sebastian, who will soon be my husband. If you seek the one you called Cesario, look behind you!"

Orsino turned
and saw Viola,
wearing a dress
that Olivia had
lent her. She
looked so lovely
that she quite took
Orsino's breath away, and he instantly
fell head over heels in love with her.

"If you take my advice, you'll marry her
straightaway," Olivia
told the Duke. "She
loves you with
all her heart!"
"And now I
see her as her
rightful self, I love
her with all mine!"
Orsino declared.

And so there was a double wedding in the house of Countess Olivia, and that night the windows were bright with lights, and the air was filled with the sounds of music and celebration.

The laughter and singing rang through the house, and reached the ears of Malvolio, who had been locked in the cellar. He pressed his face against the bars of the window and called out, "Hello, hello! Let me out, someone! I am not mad – truly I am not!"

But nobody heard him, not that night.

I'll follow this good man, and go with you,
And having sworn truth, ever will be true.

Sebastian; V.i.

Appearance in Twelfth Night

It's easy for people to get identical twins mixed up. In *Twelfth Night*, Shakespeare uses this idea with hilarious results.

Beneath the comedy, though, Shakespeare makes a serious point about how we judge people by the way they look. Viola dresses as a man, and everyone assumes that she is one. Malvolio is tricked into wearing bright yellow tights, and makes himself look ridiculous.

When Viola dresses in her brother Sebastian's clothes and pretends to be Cesario, she has no idea of what it will lead to. She falls in love with Duke Orsino, but can't tell him because he thinks that she is a man. Then Countess Olivia falls in love with Cesario, and things become *really* complicated.

Part of the fun for an Elizabethan audience came from the fact that all the female parts were played by boys. So when Viola appears as Cesario, the actor would have been a boy pretending to be a girl pretending to be a boy – as if the story weren't complicated enough!

As in most of his comedies, Shakespeare pokes fun at people in love. Orsino believes he loves Olivia, but actually he is in love with being in love. When Olivia falls for Cesario, she is transformed from a sensible, independent young woman to a lovesick teenager.

Shakespeare shows how misleading appearances can be, and that what is in peoples' hearts is far more important than the clothes they wear.

Shakespeare and the Globe Theatre

Some of Shakespeare's most famous plays were first performed at the Globe Theatre, which was built on the South Bank of the River Thames in 1599.

Going to the Globe was a different experience from going to the theatre today. The building was roughly circular in shape, but with flat sides: a little like a doughnut crossed with a fifty-pence piece. Because the Globe was an open-air theatre, plays were only put on during daylight hours in spring and summer. People paid a penny to stand in the central space and watch a play, and this part of the audience became known as 'the groundlings' because they stood on the ground. A place in the tiers of seating beneath the thatched roof, where there was a slightly better view and less chance of being rained on, cost extra.

The Elizabethans did not bath very often and the audiences at the Globe were smelly. Fine ladies and gentlemen in the more expensive seats sniffed perfume and bags of sweetly-scented herbs to cover the stink rising from the groundlings.

There were no actresses on the stage; all the female characters in Shakespeare's plays would have been acted by boys, wearing wigs and make-up. Audiences were not well-behaved. People clapped and cheered when their favourite actors came on stage; bad actors were jeered at and sometimes pelted with whatever came to hand.

Most Londoners worked hard to make a living and in their precious free time they liked to be entertained. Shakespeare understood the magic of the theatre so well that today, almost four hundred years after his death, his plays still cast a spell over the thousands of people that go to see them.

Orchard Classics
Shakespeare Stories

RETOLD BY ANDREW MATTHEWS
ILLUSTRATED BY TONY ROSS

As You Like It	978 1 84616 187 2	£4.99
Hamlet	978 1 84121 340 8	£4.99
A Midsummer Night's Dream	978 1 84121 332 3	£4.99
Antony and Cleopatra	978 1 84121 338 5	£4.99
The Tempest	978 1 84121 346 0	£4.99
Richard III	978 1 84616 185 8	£4.99
Macbeth	978 1 84121 344 6	£4.99
Twelfth Night	978 1 84121 334 7	£4.99
Henry V	978 1 84121 342 2	£4.99
Romeo & Juliet	978 1 84121 336 1	£4.99
Much Ado About Nothing	978 1 84616 183 4	£4.99
Othello	978 1 84616 184 1	£4.99
Julius Caesar	978 1 40830 506 5	£4.99
King Lear	978 1 40830 503 4	£4.99
The Merchant of Venice	978 1 40830 504 1	£4.99
The Taming of the Shrew	978 1 40830 505 8	£4.99

Orchard Books are available from all good bookshops.